Pi

A Young Lad
Goes to Sea

Pip Burke

Pip Burke

DEDICATION

To my six (so far) little grandkids; Laurie, Sid, Billy, Bobby, Alfie, and Bella, who can read this later, having told me "No, no, Grandad, not your bedtime sea stories, read us Thomas The Tank or Peppa Pig!"

PROLOGUE

"A Young Lad Goes to Sea". But why? What makes someone decide terra firm should be replaced by the pitch and roll of a ship out on the Ocean. Often, I was asked that question and the simple answer to that is - there isn't one!

Not one singular thing springs to mind so could it be an accumulation of things? Could it have come from a movie, TV or books maybe? Some say the sea is in a person's blood.

But how does it get there in the first place, especially when it doesn't run in the family? Well, not quite, with my 'old man' serving on the Hunt class Destroyer H.M.S. Cotswold during the Second World War, knowing little of these few years hadn't left me with any burning ambition to follow suit.

So, its elsewhere one has to look and going back through my childhood years seems to reveal as good as an explanation as anything with a lot of time revolving around water. Born in York inside the city walls between Fishergate and Walmgate and though 40 miles from the nearest coastline we had the next best thing; two rivers virtually on our doorstep!

With no computers or multi-channel TV's it would be fair to say the 1950's early 60's kids were definitely of the outdoor mold making much of their fun with whatever came to hand. Kids will always be attracted to water and with the rivers Ouse and Foss all but a few minutes' walk away, it was a ready-made playground for all.

Learning to swim at an early age opened up a whole new world. In winter it would be St Georges baths-hoping to outsmart 'muscle man' the lifeguard and overstay your half hour by as long as you could!

Come summer it would be long sessions at Rowntree's open-air pool or better still for some, the freedom of the river Ouse. Many a lad from around the city would have their own special riverside spots and if they weren't swimming in it, they would be fishing it. The lure of the water was just too good to miss be it inland or out on the coast in the sea. With trips to the coast few and far between the rivers were an ideal substitute for the sea which was only topped when building the university at Heslington. Digging out for the largest plastic bottom lake in Europe, when the builders went home the kids moved in!

Constructing rafts of all shapes and sizes, great times were had sailing to imaginary exotic lands. Could this then have been the moment I decided to later do it for real? For an impressionable ten-year-old yes, maybe, but a more likely scenario would come two years later with an introductory visit to the York Sea Cadet H.Q. in Micklegate. It didn't take long to realize this was the real deal, being shown and told what this well-run national organization had to offer.

That first night turned into four years…. now where do I find my first ship?

No, not my prison number..! In National Sea Training School battledress uniform for official photograph for Seaman's ID card.

CHAPTER 1: BACK TO SCHOOL AGAIN!

It was early December 1968 the Royal Docks London and my first ship the 11,000-ton 512-foot M.V. Cretic.

It would be fair to say I was a little nervous of what's in store for the next 4 months or so as the Shaw Savill line refrigerated cargo ship was set to sail to the other side of the world.

Now exactly 50 years to the month since boarding a train to London and onto the National Sea Training school at Gravesend the time had now come to put memories into print before they disappear altogether like a ship going over the horizon!

Standing on a dock in front of ships tied up stem to stern was not that unusual for me, only this time I didn't have my sea cadet mates with me. Would the next few years be as good as the last 4 years I had spent in the cadets? one could only hope so, but one thing I did know was the cadets had given me the perfect grounding for the step up to the big time!

Everything from boat handling to firing 303

rifles was on the agenda. School holidays couldn't come quick enough as week-long courses at Royal Navy bases throughout the U.K. Were eagerly booked and the icing on the cake, trips aboard warships at sea! Many a schoolmate would mock the fact that we were playing sailors but if only they knew what they were missing!

Twice weekly was cadet's night with most aspects of navy life covered like rope work, knots, hitches, splices to the more technical like wireless telegraphy. Drill and discipline were also important parts of cadet life but so too was the enjoyment of sport. How many non-cadets could say at the age of 14 or 15 that they could be in a boxing tournament one week, in a shooting competition the next, rugby 7 a-sides, boat handling and sailing regatta's, definitely nothing to ridicule in my book!

It certainly was a full calendar being in the cadets, but it didn't finish there. Many a weekend we could be either using the cadets camping gear and boats and off we would go up the river Ouse or on the North York Moors-minus adult instructors!

Ironically it would be through the sea cadets that my

next step up would come and a life-long love of sailing.

Having won through the zone and area finals in West Yorkshire our three-man crew were through to the Nationals at H.M.S. Excellent, Portsmouth. This however coincided with me joining the Merchant Navy of which I had special dispensation through both parties to take part.

Finally as we more than met our match in Portsmouth I'll say no more, but why you may ask did I join the Merchant instead of the Royal? Simple; the exam!

Having left Danesmead Secondary at 14 (my 15th was in the August summer holidays) it was to York Tech College I went on a yearlong junior builder's course taking in such trades as plumbing, joinery, bricklaying etc. As the course was nearing its end our class tutor would call each one of us to the front and ask what trade we would be going into and have we signed up to an employer. One by one the lads would step forward until the call for Burke to step to the front.

"Right." Said Mr. Lupton. "And what are you

going for young man? And have you acquired an apprenticeship?"

"No sir," said I. "I've decided to join the Royal Navy instead."

To which a bemused Mr. Lupton said, "You may not know this young man but there is no requirement for bricklayers on Aircraft Carriers!"

With the course over, it was next stop Hull to the Royal Navy careers office for first interview which didn't get off to the best of starts. It was just a short walk from my house to York railway station and onto the train to Hull. Well, that is where I thought it was going but somehow, I ended up in Leeds! The only way now is a train back to York, change, then on to Hull.

This was going to make me well late for my interview, so I rang the navy office to tell them I was stuck in Leeds. "It says here you are from York, why are you in Leeds?" came the reply.

"Sorry, but got on the wrong train," which didn't look good or go down well at the other end especially as I was going for the post of Artificer or Junior Officer! Finally arriving at the career's office and apologies over, my interviewee handed me three sets of last entrants exam papers and asked me to read through them to gauge what chance I would have of passing bearing in mind I only needed 40% in each of the subjects.

"Erm," I thought... English should be ok, Math's yes with a struggle, but Science - not a hope in hell!

Back came the grumpy Petty Officer who asked me how I would have got on.

"Not a chance with the Science," I told him.

"Well just wait a minute, let's have another look at that paper," he replied. First two questions had me shaking my head in total bewilderment, so he picked another at random and said, "Explain Archimedes Principle."

"Sorry can't," said I. So, he gave me a clue saying he was famous for saying the word Eureka!

"Ah yes, I've heard of that but still haven't a clue."

"Think, lad! He jumped into a bath and screamed Eureka! So why did he say it?"

"Ah yes, it must have been because the water was

too hot!" His face said it all as he sunk his shaking head into his hands saying, "Didn't they teach you anything at your school!?"

With the interview coming to an end he suggested I go back to York library swot up on a few science books and return for the next but one exam in 3 months' time. Having agreed to this I decided to fill the rest of the day in with a walk down the docks arriving back in York early evening to find that the Hull police had contacted their York counterparts and called at our family home.

"Does an Alan Burke live here?" they asked my mother.

"Yes, he does but he isn't here now," she replied.

"Well do you know where he is this moment in time?"

She said "No," and before she could tell them I'd gone to Hull, they said they had found documents on Hull docks with a reason to believe I could be attempting to stow away on a ship! How they came to that conclusion lord only knows other than putting two and two together and getting five!!

Just one visit to the library was enough to

convince me that schooling myself was a big no no and the dizzy heights of junior officer was maybe a bit beyond me.

A swift return to Hull to tell them of my decision didn't go down well especially when I refused their new offer of joining on the bottom rung as a rating. Switching to the more relaxed Merchant Navy office, an interview and exam was completed with ease and my intended sea career was up and running once more.

It was the summer of 1968, six days after my 16th birthday, case packed, leaving behind parents and four sisters for the journey to London and onto the National Sea Training School at Gravesend. Replacing the old Vindicatrix school this new Merchant Navy establishment was one impressive set-up on the banks of the Thames. Several hundred trainees would go through the school at a time and it wouldn't be long before new pals were made.

Our class was some 18 strong with lads from all over the U.K., the vast majority of them not knowing one end of a ship from another! Overall, they were a good set of lads but in the age of football hooliganism we unfortunately had to suffer two. Both West Ham supporters they just loved aggro with the northern lads from the likes of Liverpool, Manchester and Leeds.

Coming from York with a team in the lower reaches could have been my savior but more likely it was helping them with their rope work as it was a wonder they could even tie their bovver boot laces.

With budding trainee shipmates class Q3 Gravesend,
November 1968

Half way through the course the sad news of my gran's death came through and home I returned for her funeral, only on arriving back to find my locker broken into, though strangely nothing had gone missing!

By now I had palled on with Taffy from another class, a great guy and we quickly hit it off; hit being the optimum word here! Recalling our times back home I told him of my days in the cadets and being undefeated in two boxing bouts of which he said he had donned the gloves a time or two before.

"That's it," said Taff. "Let's put our names down on boxing night." Off we went to see the P.T.I. but to our disbelief he wouldn't sanction the fight as we were not an even match; I at five foot five were too tall and too heavy for Taff! Yep, he was a little wisp of a lad was Taff!

Pleading with the P.T.I. to let two pals in the ring together he said there could be a way, but it would have to be done on the quiet. It could go ahead under the guise of a grudge fight which basically is when two guys are caught fighting by the staff and given the offer of finishing it off in the ring over three rounds but nobody being judged a winner at the end to prevent the feud continuing.

Great, now all we had to do was fake a fight

within the grounds, get caught by a member of staff then the bout was on. The rigged fight though well-rehearsed resembled more of a wrestling match as we both didn't want to hurt each other, which came to an end when staff stepped in, the main thing though was we were now set for the ring!

Come Mondays boxing night we were on the end of the bill with me thinking "Is this fair?" and feeling rather guilty of knocking hell out of my little chum. At the sound of the bell I strode to the centre of the ring to be met by a constant barrage of jabs to the head and hooks to the body with proper skillful boxing shots thinking "What the hell's happening here!? Somebody is taking the piss!" This fella can not only box but is bloody good and far too good for me as I somehow saw out the 1st round.

Hardly into the 2nd and another punch I never saw coming landed smack on the nose and as the blood started to run the ref had seen enough and stopped it.

 With the bout over and shaking hands in the middle I said, "Where the hell did that come from!"

"Forgot to tell you Pip, I've fought in the Welsh

A.B.A's." Yep, I was well and truly had but at least we still stayed pals!

When I was in the cadets I finished as one of the oldest AB's never to get promotion to leading seaman mainly due to messing about too much . With this in mind I vowed that when I get to sea school things will be different, taking a more serious attitude and in sharp contrast to my secondary school days was now up at the top end of the class, if not the top!

This new line of thinking reaped its rewards when I was chosen to represent the Merchant Navy on their float in the Lord Mayor of London's annual parade. Into the last week and a few bob was to be earned drawing anchors on newly purchased canvas kit bags which the school were selling, with many believing if you are going to be a sailor then you may as well look like one!

CHAPTER 2:
FINALLY UNDERWAY

On the train homeward and never been out of the U.K. before, thoughts turned to where I could be heading in a few weeks' time. America, Africa, Far East, Australia even, wondering if I will get a choice or that the first trip is already mapped out for me.

Three weeks at home then another train to Hull, hoping it's not going to be as eventful as last time and onto the British Shipping Federation, aka the 'Pool' office down Posterngate. The Hull Pool was the seaman's equivalent of the employment office in civvy street.

A board on the wall full of ships like tankers, passenger liners, general cargo stating destination, crew required, length of voyage, departure date all you need to know with the only problem being which one do I pick? Many would tick the box for any first tripper but one in particular would stand out, the M.V. Cretic a four and a bit month trip to New Zealand calling at Fiji on the way out and various ports in the Mediterranean on the way back.

This sounded more like a free luxury cruise with the only difference being they were going to pay me for doing it!

With my new canvas bag which resembled an oversize duffle bag on my shoulder I must have looked like Popeye heading towards York station wondering if 'Pipeye' would make a more appropriate nickname!

The journey down to London posed no problems having done it several times before in the cadets only the Royal Docks where Cretic was berthed was new to me. New also was boarding the ships gangway and thinking "Where do I go and who do I see?" Especially with the ship crawling with dockers loading the holds with cargo.

It wasn't long before I was shown to my cabin, a small compact room on the working deck with double bunk, set of drawers, built in wardrobe and day bed/settee across the end of the cabin in front of the proverbial porthole. This will do I thought but a bit small for two that changed back to one when the chief steward said the top bunk will remain empty. "So spread yer wings, lad you've got it all to yourself."

It wasn't till the following day when more crew started to sign on did I get to find out a little of just who was who. There would be around 16 or so ratings to work the deck department. Able Seaman, Efficient Deck Hands, Senior Ordinary Seaman, Junior Ordinary Seaman and at the bottom, me, Deck Boy.

Another night in port brought several of the crew plus myself together in the bakers cabin and a first tasting of Tennants canned beer. At this time beer was far from my favourite tipple, much preferring a pint of milk instead, but it was a good excuse to sit and mix with new shipmates who were full of tales of what ships they had been on but basically just friendly chit chat. All this was proving a good ice breaker but that was all to change when the baker who was obviously gay asked me how old I was.

When I replied 16, out of earshot of the others he whispered in my ear, "That's old enough, I'll have you before this trip is out!"

Knowing exactly what he meant I moved away, stood by the now packed cabin door for a while longer before disappearing back to my cabin and locking the door. It was a long night and I hardly slept a wink!.

The following lunchtime we were finally underway with all my thoughts centered on the baker and how the hell am I going to evade him for four months!

The initial romance of adventure had now been severely dented as we sailed down the Thames passing Gravesend Sea School before hard a starboard and out into the English Channel. Now in the world's busiest sea lanes ships going up and down, ferries back and forth were of little concern to me as my first day at sea took on another shattering blow… sea sickness! Maybe I should change that to home sickness as I started to question myself as to had I made the right decision of a life at sea! The sickness was uncontrollable, making a mess wherever I went, in the accommodation alleyways, my cabin, out on deck and the only person to clear it up was me!

I was told in no uncertain terms to stop wandering round the ship leaving my calling card in my wake, which was only achieved when they lashed my hands to the leeward rails to ride the sickness out and eventually… Bingo!... it worked, and I was never to suffer it ever again!

One problem solved, a second soon followed when confiding with our Hull lamp trimmer on the baker threat. Just the odd word from Big Ken left the baker in no doubt that his bread making days would be over if he didn't keep away!

Three days out of London, still working out who's who, one asks am I the skipper's son and another saying surely I can't be the deck boy as I don't look old enough. I was now 16 years and 3 months, but many thought a good few years younger as we headed towards the Panama Canal and the Pacific Ocean.

The routine of life on board was now settling down, every morning looking after the P.O.'s as Petty Officers Peggy, then out working on deck in the afternoon. The 12 weeks at sea school had been a good grounding but the 4 years previous in the York sea cadets can't be overstated as I began to take to life at sea like the proverbial duck to water. Work at sea was 7 days a week, Monday to Friday the standard 8 hours plus 3 hours per day overtime, and overtime Saturday and Sunday. This sounds like a top-heavy workload but when you are living and working on the job its surprising just how much free time you have. That time could be spent in many ways and with no mother to do it for you, washing, drying, ironing your clothes, doing the bed, and cleaning the cabin. You had to grow up fast and it was definitely the making of me!

On the leisure front, the crew bar was a popular place with dominoes, darts, and crib competitions often taking place with the ale coming from the ships bond; though alas not for underage me. Officially unable to purchase beer I didn't go without when I finally decided I quite liked the taste; the older guys saw to that! Sickness and the baker saga behind me, I was without doubt now enjoying life at sea and knew I had made the right decision. Glad also I'd chosen the "merch" over the stricter royal.

My first ship, M.V. Cretic off the coast of New Zealand

CHAPTER 3:
MULES OF PANAMA

Slowly but surely, I began to put names to faces and faces to jobs and for first tripper Burke, some comedian gave me the unwanted nickname of Tiny Tim.

"What's wrong with my original nickname of Pip?" I thought. Taking an instant dislike to that only made things worse when some shortened it to Tim and when it went even a step further to Timmy... I thought I'd become the ships cat!

Before the canal was a bunkering visit to Curacao but sadly not long enough time for a first run ashore – not even for a cat!

Underway again and a short run to the gateway of the Pacific, the Panama Canal where we would have to wait along with several other ships to pass through, but first going to anchor.

At least it was now Christmas Day! Though Santa had forgot to drop some presents down our funnel the festive day was much the same it would be back in York except for seeing a pod of whales heading north. Yep, that's something they won't see in the Ouse back home!

Knowing little of the history behind the building of the Canal except that thousands of workers had died constructing it, I had to rely on what the old boys told me. To get the ships through, mules are used to keep the ships central in the locks and any spare food for these hard-working animals is gratefully accepted. Step in Tiny. Yes, under sufferance I had now accepted my new adopted nickname and had previously collected two large sacks of old or discarded bread buns I'd been saving for this purpose.

As we approached the first lock the bosun turned us out on deck ready to accept the lines from the mules that only I couldn't see. "But where are they Bo, aren't they here yet?" I asked.

"There lad . Those box engines on tracks are called Mules so you better dump all that bloody bread - the buggers have done yer!"

After feeling glad that at least I didn't have to feed some poor emaciated mules, I actually had to laugh myself. I was still annoyed that I'd been had as I vowed no one would catch me out as I had been previously well versed on the tricks the crew would play on a first tripper.

A tight squeeze for two ships going through the canal.

With the bread buns put aside, maybe for a treat for the Pacific fish, all eyes were now on the open gates of Gatun Lock. These massive concrete structures had chambers over 300 metres long doubled up so two ships could pass simultaneously in opposite directions. After exiting the lock and entering the lakes and cuts it would be another 8 hours or so before Miraflores Lock and out into the Pacific Ocean.

Marveling at this engineering feat saving shipping thousands of miles from going around Cape Horn, down at the stern of the ship sat a few Greasers having a smoko break from work down the engine room.

"Are you into fishing Tiny?" said one.

"Yea, used to do quite a bit with me cousin back home in the local rivers."

"Well here, we've made this hook and line so go get a chunk of meat from the galley and bobs yer uncle."

Not needing a rod, they paid out the baited line over the stern and left me to it, as they disappeared back to work down below.

As I sat there taking in the scenery waiting for my first bite thinking this is some view compared with an early Sunday morning start sat down fishing in the Foss Basin back in York, the first of many would come by and ask-"Is there owt doing?"

"No not yet," would come my repetitive reply as I sat, and sat, and sat knowing fishing is a waiting game but now time was beginning to drag. As more interested watchers passed my way, a chuckle here and a grin there started to get me thinking that something isn't quite right here!

"Bloody hell," it finally clicked. The turbulence and sound of our twin screws was probably scaring every sodding fish for miles!

Done again! Two nil to them!

The now open season of 'get Tiny the greenhorn first tripper' swung temporarily my way when refusing to go for 'a long stand'. C'mon lads you can do better than that! More would be coming my way for sure but with an already decent understanding of nautical terminology there would bound to be plenty I didn't know about.

Ships going through Miraflores Lock, assisted by the Mules though definitely not powered by bread buns!

CHAPTER 4:
FIRST STEP ASHORE FIJI

The British winter was now but a distant memory with boots and t-shirts the daily attire and a basic wage of £25 per month, nearly doubling that with overtime. I was earning a small fortune compared with apprenticeship mates back home. Yep, life was good, and I bet that some would wish they were here!

However, one wish I wasn't looking forward to was the line crossing ceremony, the initiation rite of sailors first crossing of the equator. The day was looming fast. I was one of four lined up but come the time, one went missing... me! No way did I fancy being stripped naked, covered in grease or dye, pelted with old fruit or whatever else they had in mind. It was a big ship, hiding away wasn't a problem.

Feeling quite chuffed with myself of evading King Neptune and the system, I soon had the smug smile wiped off my face when I was told by one of the 'old salts' it was done for a reason and not just for fun. The serious side being to ensure new shipmates were capable of handling rough stormy times at sea.

Sailors can be very superstitious people; it was

obvious I still had a lot to learn and now I was feeling a right prat!

On the messroom bulkhead was a map taking in our voyage that was filled in daily with an e.t.a. of forthcoming places. Next stop would be Fiji but before that Pitcairn Island, a place I just had to see.

Populated by Polynesians till the late 15th century but with natural resources running out, the island became uninhabited until they were rediscovered by Europeans. It got its name after Robert Pitcairn the 15 years old midshipman on the British sloop H.M.S. Swallow who first sighted the island back in 1767. However, it wasn't till 23 years later that it hit the headlines again when Fletcher Christian and 9 fellow mutineers of the Bounty came ashore. As we would be passing to the north of the island close enough for a photograph or two, this would be an opportunity not to be missed and an early morning shout from the watch, seeing it live as oppose to in books or the movies was a real plus.

If Christian was the bad guy then his former Captain, James Cook was his opposite. A true boyhood hero of mine, someone I now couldn't read enough about and the main reason I had become a stickler for factual books. One of these was on my little bookshelf and of course it was about Cook, but it would be awhile before I would be following in his wake – no Panama Canal in his days, he had to go the long way around!

Having departed London on the 12th December it was the 12th of January when we arrived in Fiji and its capital Suva. This would prove a first connection with Cook who would become the second European to land here in 1774, beaten by the great Dutch explorer Abel Tasman some 130 years earlier.

It was however Cook who conceived the name Fiji by differences in pronunciation from the Fijians who called it 'Viti' and the Tongans 'Fisi'.

With Cooks stay short, there was little time to record the Islands to which much credit must go down to one of his former crew Captain William Bligh who set about the task some 15 years later.

As we came alongside this was my first chance to step on terra firma since leaving London. I hadn't got far, in fact halfway down the gangway, making way for a one-armed bum boat seller on the way up. His good arm was up to the shoulder in watches and a tray with a strap around his neck full of nick-nacks looking like an ice cream seller at the pictures.

Politely turning down his offer to stop and buy, off I went in search of a beach and first dip in the Pacific Ocean. It didn't disappoint, just like a picture postcard, white sand and palm trees lapped by a sparkling blue sea.

A typical Fiji beach and a first ever dip in the Pacific Ocean

That swim could have been spoilt or not taken at all had I earlier found out how old Joe had lost his arm; munched off by a shark at the beach I had just been to!

Staying just long enough to nip ashore again, I thought I would try the local market as time I got some pressies for the girls back home. But what does a guy buy four sisters? Thinking of something traditional, the 'Fiji Fragrance' looked a bit naff and the 'Midnight in Grimsby' perfume seemed a bit fishy… Well, at least I got that gag! And I reckon they wouldn't get full use of a grass skirt each back in York, even though they were on offer of two for the price of one!

Thinking, I'll leave it till later, but if only we were going to Australia… I could have got them a boomerang each!

Now looking forward to a long stay in Auckland, our next stop, they were at it again and this time from up above! An envelope with several names written on it had to be read and signed by various members of the crew with me being the mobile postman. Off I went and in turn they would read the note inside, sign it, then on my way to the next on the list. No problem, easy enough job until I had to go down the engine room to find the storekeeper. Because of the heat and noise, the engine room was not for me. Just coming into contact with metal could leave a nasty mark on bare skin.

Back on deck the 1st mate was found, then the bosun, plus several others till back down the engine room for the fridge engineer; it seemed silly I had to do it in order written.

Beginning to smell a rat, I thought why not have a sneaky look seeing that it wasn't sealed. So, into one of the deck lockers I went, opened it and it said, 'KEEP THIS LAD MOVING'.

Sod it!. They've done me again and now the officers are at it!

CHAPTER 5: AUCKLAND'S NOT FOR SWIMMING

All good clean fun though as we homed in on the New Zealand coast line that was so accurately mapped by Cook on his first voyage that those charts were still being used in the early 1960's. The first point of land spotted on that voyage was by the 12-year-old surgeons assistant Nicholas Young and for his efforts, Cook named that point of land 'Young Nicks Head'.

"Ah," I thought, "If I spot it first this time, think I'll change the bulkhead map to 'Young Pip's Head'."

6 o'clock in the morning, it was out with the camera clicking away on the approaches to our Auckland berth which was quite a spectacular run in.

Now using a brand-new Olympus Penn automatic camera lent to me by none other than the baker, who by now I was good friends with since Ken put him in his place. Having purchased it in duty free Suva it was mine to use for the duration of the trip and costing a whopping £44, I was told to look after it!

Couldn't wait to get ashore and with the waterfront and berths at the end of Queen Street the main shopping area, it was just a short walk to town.

With the minimum age being 20 to drink in New Zealand that counted me out, but I never felt I was missing out. In fact, one of the best places to drink was our own crew bar, especially as I would find out here in Kiwi.

"How about a walk ashore to meet some nice girls' lads?" said Paddy.

"I think pubs are out," replied Stu the galley boy.

"We aint going to the pub, we're off to Woolies. Yes, the same Woolworths as back home."

Typical Irish blarney I thought, he's got to be having a laugh, can't be, we are on the other side of the world for god's sake! Sure as eggs are eggs, we walked through the doors and could easily have been in Woolworths Coney St in York!

"Hello Paddy, nice to see you back again,"

"Yea, it's good to be back Helen. Fancy coming aboard tonight? I can leave some passes at the gate."

"Had nothing planned for tonight so yea, that will be good Paddy. Will round up the gang and see you later then."

Wandering around the store, the waves and winks Paddy was getting off the girls showed he had certainly been here before; four times in fact. He definitely knew the score!

A cultural trip to the Maori museum filled in the rest of the afternoon then back to the ship and into the bar. Our Woolies girls duly arrived, and the crew bar was soon full of life, a real let your hair down sort of place, in total contrast to the officers 'be on your best behavior bar.'

With enough bottles of Lion bitter to sink a battle ship, one would never go short of a drink and it wasn't long before I hit it off with Sue who worked the Woolies sweet counter. Good looking and good company with a wicked sense of humour, before she left she asked me, would I like to come and visit her at her parent's house the next night?

Taking up her offer, I took a taxi out into the suburbs arriving at a detached chalet type house to be met by Sue who said her parents were soon going out for the night and ushered me into her bedroom.

The first thing that struck me was photos of

ships all around the top of her bedroom wall. "What's all that about?" I thought, as her parents left and in came four of her friends. All was soon revealed, telling me they just loved going on British ships with the photos being like a picture record of such.

Drinking and chatting away the girls were starting to come across as very streetwise and appearing older than they actually were.

"Do you fancy a swim Pip" said Sue showing me the outdoor pool through her bedroom window.

"Aw, I wish you had told me before I left then I could have brought me trunks." With that they all burst out laughing.

"What's so funny with that?" I asked.

"You don't need trunks. We would all skinny dip, silly."

Gobsmacked! I could sense myself going as red as a beetroot. They really meant it and the embarrassment must have been written all over my face. I was now feeling well out of my comfort zone and found it hard to make conversation from then on.

Eventually I made an excuse and said I had to go

on watch at midnight so had to leave. This lame excuse I'm sure was picked up from the girls as I bid my farewell. Back on board I thought "Jesus, can't tell the guys about this, they will think I've got a slate loose!"

Our outward stay in Auckland had come to an end and on the way down to Dunedin, I was surprised to see two women still on board who were shacking up with two AB's. As long as they were kept out of sight of the officers above, this was apparently quite common with British ships visiting Kiwi and with a return to Auckland in 5 days' time, a little cruise for the girls and no doubt a bit of enjoyment for the guys.

The Maori and the first sighting of New Zealand coast line – no wonder Captain Cook was reluctant to step ashore!

CHAPTER 6: ALBATROSS ALERT!

Now down in the South Island, Paddy again showing all the qualities of a tour rep suggested a few of us go horse riding in the hills. Having first told him no, as the only four-legged thing that I had been on before was a Scarborough donkey, he somehow convinced me to give it a go.

Arriving at the stables he told me to say I had ridden before or I wouldn't be allowed out of the paddock and into the hills. Panic set in when I saw the size of my steed and in front of everyone I put my wrong foot in the stirrup, only getting away with it when Paddy said, "Don't take any notice of him he's always clowning around."

Finally mounted, the stable girls were giving me funny looks and must have known I was as green as grass when it came to horsemanship. After a short while we set off at a walk out of the paddock, heading for the open ground with Paddy giving me constant instructions on how to handle the beast.

"Let's get a move on Tiny, give it some heel," he said, but nothing happened!

"Harder," he shouted, eventually turning back to give its rear a whack only for the bloody thing to take off! Now totally out of control galloping across the fields heading straight for a wood, pulling on the reins but obviously not hard enough, the horse spotted a slight gap, shooting into it.

As I shut my eyes, branches and bracken were scratching me everywhere till the spooked horse finally came to a stop when it couldn't go any further into the wood… and thank God it did because I couldn't stop it!

I thought "Sod Paddy's days out, I'm off back." There being met by the girls who didn't need an excuse why I was back so soon, I reckon they saw it all!

When I was at sea school one of the instructors gave us a bit of advice saying take some things from home; nick-nacks, something personal like photos, anything that could help first trippers over homesickness. Not wanting to overload my kit bag I decided on rugby league programmes of which I was an ardent collector.

Though it may seem odd to some, one from each

of the 30 pro clubs stuck around my cabin worked as it gave colour as much as anything else and not cumbersome to take back.

Yes, that reminded me, must not forget some pressies for the family! Leaving that job till the last day in Dunedin; in fact that late I nearly missed the ships departure, arriving back at the berth with the gangway raised a couple of feet off the dock, a sign that no more allowed ashore or aboard as the ship is now due to sail.

As I jumped the gap to the gangway, Ken the lampy was waiting up top and gave me the biggest bollocking. Not just for nearly missing the boat but he wanted me to meet a docker from Hull who emigrated out to Kiwi and had played professional rugby league with my 'old man.'

A half back with Hull K. R. they were both in the side that took on the 1948 Australian tourists at Craven Park and with Burke junior nowhere to be found Ken's only offer of a connection with the past was to show him my cabin resplendent in rugby programmes!

He wasn't a happy chappy and neither was the

old man when I eventually told him when back home!

Heading back to Auckland, on the approach to our berth, word got around that one of the crew fueled by drink had been throwing empty beer bottles at an alleged injured Albatross floating on the water, with an excuse it was a humane act to put the bird out of its misery.

Whether this was true or not it stirred up much anger amongst the older 'salts' on board.

Not knowing much about the birds or what they stood for, I was soon put in the picture saying they represented the souls of lost seaman. Harming them would bring bad luck to the point of death on board or, worse still, ships going to the bottom with all hands!

The more I listened, the more I couldn't help thinking is there really something in this superstitious stuff that you could only mock in front of these guys at your peril.

First night back, I wondered if I would be seeing the Woolies girls but secretly wishing and hoping they have moved on to other ships in port.

My wish would be gratefully granted saving me

further embarrassment and ridicule from the guys as probably the only sailor alive who would refuse a dip with five nude good-looking girls!

As our bar started to fill, in strode half a dozen Maori girls, some well-known to the lads having been on the Cretic previously, with one in particular standing out; and not just for her extra-large size!

Big Flo was a lesbian who had spent some time in prison, for what am not sure, but she was undoubtably the boss of the group and well known on British ships.

It soon became clear why she was so popular in crew bars; a great voice and guitar player who I would take to straight away and her to me, but more I suspect in a motherly sort of way. Another of her group also caught my eye but this time for her looks - an attractive girl of Maori mother and English father called Patti.

With that awkward non-swim night behind me this was much more to my liking and comfort as we got on like a house on fire. So much so that I asked her if she fancied a stroll down to my cabin (to see my rugby programmes of course) and she was that impressed she decided to stay the night!

With a chill in the air next morning I lent her a jumper that was given to me by a Gravesend instructor and off I went to a pre-arranged boat trip around Auckland Harbour. Taking the posh baker's camera with me, the automatic view finder was proving a right nuisance. If the light wasn't good enough it wouldn't let you take the picture which was annoying me more and more especially as I was trying to get some shots of a yacht race taking place. With the camera strap getting in the way when leaning over the boats side rails, for some dumb reason I took the strap off my neck then the next thing... BANG! My elbow struck a stanchion on the boat and I dropped the bloody camera over the side!

"No!" I screamed as it sank to the bottom of Auckland Harbour.

What the hell am I gonna do now? What's he going to say when I tell him I've lost his new camera that he still hasn't used? This is going to take a massive chunk out of my pay.... Well, that's when I pluck up enough courage to tell him that is!

Returning to the ship thinking things couldn't get

any worse, sods law it did when Patti was nowhere to be seen. Neither was my jumper and a missing pair of Levi jeans. With three days left before leaving Kiwi, I thought little of it and that she would return.

"Don't hold yer breath," said Paddy. "Looks like the Maoris are still at it then Tiny, still nicking stuff from sailors like the days of yer Captain Cook!"

Even worse news came the following night when several crew off a British Blue Star boat came aboard with their deck boy telling me of a Gravesend instructor who had recently died. It only happened to be the one who gave me the gansey! Now I just had to get it back, if not just for sentimental reasons!

Rumor was rife that two of the crew had, or were about to, 'jump ship' and stay behind in New Zealand with two schools of thought; women or superstition. Jumping ship for a life in another country though illegal was not uncommon and according to the 'old salts', neither was superstition and the dead Albatross. Surely not I thought!

Into the last night in Auckland, no sign of Patti and though several women came aboard, no Flo either.

One of the girls promised to get a message to Flo about Patti and my missing gear saying she will sort it and see you next trip.

Tugs alongside, gangway up and we were on our way, though two crew light. There was word from the lower deck that they had gone off with two women with most believing it a honey trap, as money could be earned for handing in deserting seaman.

Ships berthed alongside Auckland's waterfront.

CHAPTER 7:
BACK TO NORMALITY

In some ways it was good to get back to sea and the routine and normality of shipboard life. Having kept my work sheets, now exactly 50 years old, its easy and interesting to look back and re- live life back then.

Deck work could be varied daily but outward much time was spent maintaining the rigging and homeward you would soon become an expert with a paint brush!

Heading north eastwards, no stopping now till we reach the canal again, a visitor joined us over the stern. This time a 'live' Albatross, the world's largest living bird. This was a first for me watching this huge bird glide effortlessly on wind drafts off the waves. 'Albert Ross', as our flying friend is otherwise affectionately called by some mariners, is a bird of many contradictions and tales, bringing good or bad luck its way.

For a first tripper like myself, any story was worth listening to when told by the old boys, some leaving lasting impressions. One such was if this wanderer of the Oceans was to land on the ship a death would occur and if it should land on the masthead then the ship would go down with all hands!

Did 1 believe this? Well, let's say enough for me to check first thing every morning that 'Albert' was there over the stern and nowhere else!

During the night hours a watch system is in place with an officer on the bridge accompanied by a rating who would act as lookout from one of three places; the bow, wing of the bridge or monkey island (above the bridge). It took just one incident to set the superstitious 'Albert' rumors going when the officer of the watch asked who was wandering about above on the monkey island in the dead of night when the watch had never left the bridge wing and everyone else other than down the engine room were tucked up in their bunks!

A second inexplicable event followed the next night, though on a different watch with different watchkeepers. Around four in the morning in the middle of a calm Pacific Ocean they swore they heard a dog barking!

Was this just a wind up or were they mistaken in what they had heard? One thing for sure, there was no mistake with 'Alberts' whereabouts. He'd vanished from the stern but, more importantly, was not on the masthead or ship as a whole!

"The signs are all there. Bad luck is coming our way and it's got nothing to do with coming in threes," said old Geordie Sam on his last trip to sea. Little would I know or believe, that bad luck would come later and in particular… to me!

Out on deck, anything and everything that didn't move was getting a coat of paint and any chance to go aloft in a bosuns chair I was at the front of the queue. Approaching the canal the weather was very hot and we were thankful of the forward motion of the ship to create a welcome breeze. Up I went the forward mast some 50 feet or so above the deck with my pot of buff paint tied to the chair thinking this is by far the hottest time I've ever tried to put paint on metal. I can't have put many brushfuls on before the sky changed from blue to grey and in what seemed like an instant, the heavens opened!

"Get down sharpish," shouted the bosun as the

rain hammered down so hard it felt like hailstones lashing my back. Inching my way down bit by bit I touched down on the deck as the sky started to change once again and as quickly as it started it finished. The deluge coming to an end, sun coming out to dry the already hot deck so fast that steam was rising everywhere!

Whenever it rains hard now I think back to that mother of all cloud bursts and can easily understand how they suffer severe weather in that part of the world.

Out of Miraflores lock and into the lake, the job of the day was to hose down the boat deck housing using fresh water from the lake ready for painting... a good excuse for a water fight or what!?

One thing the bosun forgot to stress was to keep the hoses off the hot funnel... too late! As layers of old paint came slicing off in huge sheets!

"You stupid buggers not the bloody funnel! Haven't you any sense? Well hot or not you'll get up there and repaint the bugger before we get out of this canal." And what a nightmare job it was! The heat was intense going up the inside of the funnel then slinging stages and bosun's chairs over the top. Hastily made knee pads had only little effect repelling the heat that even came through the toe ends of our boots that were in contact with the funnel.

The paint went on like grease as it was virtually drying before it left the rollers! The sooner we got the job done the better and it certainly wasn't worth the fun of a water fight!

Gatun lock and the Atlantic beckoned having steamed 6,500 miles from Auckland and the 51 mile stretch of the canal. Opened in 1914 saving 8,000 miles of going around Cape Horn it is without doubt one of the world's greatest engineering feats.

Built at a great cost to human life with yellow fever and malaria killing some 20,000 workers, at times more than 40,000 were employed on the project digging and cutting their way through, plus building the great locks that were needed to lift the ships up an incredible 26 metres!

All this left a lasting impression as I was fortunate to traverse the canal on another four more later occasions, the last being just as inspiring as the first!

Passing through the locks often brought all and sundry out on deck watching and photographing the mules doing their work; one which was our baker who asked me how his camera was performing. Still not daring to tell him or anyone else in fact, I made an excuse that I had taken enough photos on my own camera on the way out. Whether he could detect the worry on my face lord only knows but I couldn't bring myself to tell him his posh camera was no more!

Having left the Pacific saying temporary farewell to Cook and all he discovered and charted, a word must be said for another famous British seafarer, Sir Francis Drake who was buried here at sea off the Panama coast as we now headed east into the Atlantic.

Some 5,800 miles lay ahead before reaching our next port of call Piraeus, Greece and it wasn't long before we had the company of another Albatross. This time however it appeared more menacing in flight, flying much closer to the stern of the ship as though it was looking for a suitable place to land!

Word soon got around that people were feeding it tit bits but somehow it got misinterpreted to throwing things at it and with the Auckland bird attack still fresh in some minds, the inevitable had to happen; another fall out within the crew but this time on a bigger scale.

It was during a session on the beer that things finally came to a head. With tempers frayed, several of the greasers walked out of the crew bar leaving a soured atmosphere that wouldn't heal for the rest of the voyage.

Any accident however small down the engine room was now being blamed on bad luck and the bird, though conversely laughed at by some of the deck guys who equally rubbished the previous episodes of the dog barking and ghostly footsteps above the bridge.

Was this finally approaching payback time for ship and crew? Would this huge bird be about to land on board and bring about bad luck or disaster for all? Or is it really only silly superstition passed down through time?

One thing that couldn't be questioned is the stats that go with this incredible bird of the oceans. With its 3.5 metre wingspan, it's the largest living bird on the planet that can soar for several hours without flapping its wings. They are so efficient at flying they can actually use up less energy in the air than they would sitting on the nest.

In the air they have no peers with a Wandering Albatross tracked at flying a staggering 6,000 km in just 12 hours. By virtue of its size and time spent in flight it has no natural predators, enjoying a life span of up to 60 years! How the old mariners in Cooks days would have loved a life span like that!

The Albatross. The world's largest living bird... friend or foe?

The once relaxed, easy-going atmosphere on the outward leg had amongst some turned strained to say the least, with several refusing to acknowledge each other. This was awkward times for me who had to work between the two and inadvertently set the cat amongst the pigeons again at breakfast in the mess room. When asked to pass the salt pot, I handed it to old Sam who told me to put it down first, snapping at me saying "You don't ever pass it hand to hand, its bloody bad luck."

Trying to laugh it off just made matters worse when one of the AB's told him to "leave the lad alone you stupid old prat."

That was it, up shot Sam sending his chair flying. This superstitious stuff was certainly hitting a nerve or two and it could only get worse, which it inevitably did the very next morning. Awoken earlier than usual due to the rocking motion of the ship, a glance through the porthole confirmed a weather change from blue sky to angry grey.

Having enjoyed a relatively smooth passage so far, this for me was a welcome change. Safe in the knowledge of not being on a 17th century Square Rigger being tossed about on a wild ocean I was interested to see how my sea legs would stand up.

With sea sickness left behind in the English

Channel and no sign of it returning… stage one accomplished! Stage two… how would I fare moving about a ship tossing back and forth, pitching side to side? Well now was the time to find out, as it looks like we are in for rough weather!

With very few up and about, first job was to check on the bird and there it was like the two previous days, gliding effortlessly over the stern as though it was dismissing the foul weather.

By the time breakfast was over the storm had intensified, jobs out on deck were curtailed other than essential work and moving about was now proving a challenge. Lightening was flashing across the sky as the rain lashed down. We were in a proper storm!

Not being able to see the big wave hits coming, moving around the accommodation proved to be a right battle to stay on your feet, constantly bracing yourself against the bulkheads as the ship lurched from side to side.

Little if any work had been done that morning with the deck day workers enjoying an extended smoko. But not for me as the PO's mess room needing sorting and another bollocking was coming my way.

Whistling as I swayed to and fro, trying to wash the pots, the engine room store keeper asked if I was doing it on purpose just to aggravate people, reminding me of the earlier salt pot incident that upset one of his men. Oblivious as I was to know that handing a simple salt pot to someone could cause such a stink, I thought, what's wrong this time?

"What have I done now then?" I asked.

"Whistling," said he. "Don't you think we've got enough going on outside for you to take the piss and bring on more? Time you got a bloody grip lad."

No back-chat this time as I was left speechless and it was only later talking to the cook that I was told whistling was a big no-no with some, as it brings on the wind; wind we didn't need any more of!

Talk about learning the hard way! But one thing was clear; just how superstitious some sailors are and how seriously it could be taken.

The storm lasted all day and well into the early hours of next morning and I thought twice about announcing it was 'Albatross eggs on toast' for breakfast, thinking its' time to wind in my daft sense of humour for the time being!

As for our following flying friend, 'Albert Ross' stayed with us till the next day hopefully leaving us in a friendly way, something that couldn't be said for some of the crew!

CHAPTER 8:
THE MED BECKONS

Out on deck, the storm caused little damage as most things were battened down in anticipation, though the same couldn't be said for down the hatches where the 'Chippy' took charge of shoring up what got loose.

This was carpentry of the rough kind, helping him cut and nail the timber... none of that junior builders tech college detail joinery stuff needed down here!

Looking at the bulkhead map it was another long leg, nearly 4,500 miles before sighting land, that being the Straits of Gibraltar. At just 9 miles wide, we should be taking in the sights of Europe to the left and Africa to the right and never having been out of the U.K. before, another box to tick!

Work-wise I was always trying to tick as many new boxes as I could and a near constant nagging at the bosun often proved dividends. A little moan about chipping off the rust followed by a red lead undercoat and finally, a gloss coat on countless numbers of the ships rails could get a tad monotonous and more stimulating stuff was needed.

"Well, what the hell did you want to paint today?" the gaffer would sigh.

"Something more interesting and intricate would do, I can do those rails with me eyes shut now!" Came my cheeky reply.

And fair play to him; if he could oblige then he would. Out came the smaller paint brushes and any letters or figures such as FIRE, EMERGENCY EXITS, S.W.L, weight limits etc, were now being done freehand instead of using worn stencils.

Hearing the Lampy was renewing rope work on the bosun's chairs, he didn't have to ask twice for an assistant. Soon I was knocking out the completed item, maybe not as quick as him but my splices were just as correct and neat - take a bow Sea Cadets where I learnt to splice around 13 years old!

The days were now shooting by and though great credit had to be given to the cadets and sea school, there was no substitute for learning on the job. More than once I would be told: "You may have been shown that way but out here you do it this way!"

Point taken, this was indeed the real world and I couldn't get enough of it!

Approaching the Straits of Gibraltar, we were now steaming through the same waters often frequented by Britain's most famous Admiral, Horatio Nelson. To the north west is the headland of Cape Trafalgar where Nelson aboard his flagship, the 104-gun H.M.S. Victory, obliterated the combined fleets of the French and Spanish without losing a single ship of his own.

Sadly, Nelson and Britain's greatest naval victory would cost him his life that day, 21st October 1805.

Next up off the starboard side and unmissable at 1400 feet high was the 'Rock' itself, but it would be nearly another 1500 miles before striking land again and an ancient one at that; Greece.

The Rock of Gibraltar, gateway to the 'Med'.

But first it was the small matter of spanning three quarters of the 'Med', an area that had taken off as a holiday destination in the 60's but somewhere I knew little about.

After Greece it would be Italy, Cyprus then Spain, places I could only read about at school but now they were paying me to go there! One thing was for sure, I was going to make the most of it, this working holiday doesn't get better than this!

Up on the bridge giving the brass a polish up, I asked the 1st Mate what's the e.t.a. for docking in Greece.

"A long time," said he. "Think you've got your route mixed up, its Genoa next."

Admitting I'd never heard of Genoa before setting foot on this ship, he said, "Didn't you do anything on Christopher Columbus at your school, because he was born there!" If we did then it obviously hadn't stuck in my memory but it sure will now as it would be another great mariner and explorer to have been in the wake of since leaving London. Cook, Drake, Nelson and now Columbus, quite an impressive list for a first trip to sea!

So, Italy it was and their largest sea port for a stay long enough to warrant a sub on my pay and a trip ashore with our J.O.S., Tommy, a cheeky cockney who was a year or so older than me.

First impressions of Italy weren't good. Old buildings, narrow streets, looks as though it aint changed much since Columbus' days! So different from last port Auckland. Money in our pockets, off we went, and with no set route planned we headed up and away from the Docks.

The more we walked the better it got with wider roads and a more pleasant open feel to the place. Waiting to cross a road, deciding which way to go next a woman asked us if we were lost and needed some directions. Having told her no, we were just out for a general look around we ended up in a walking conversation with her as she could speak pretty good English. During this she mentioned she had even been to York, staying at the then Chase Hotel. After another fifteen minutes or so of light-hearted banter she was about to head off, then asked us if we would like to come for a coffee at her place.

"We're in here," whispered Tommy out of the

side of his mouth, but as she led us away from the main thoroughfare towards a maze of narrow lanes and tall buildings, I wasn't now so sure.

Finally, we got to a block of flats and as we went through the front door she said, "Wait here, I'll only be a minute," and started to climb the stairs of the three-story flats.

"That's it lets go," I said to Tommy. "I don't like this."

"No," he said, "She fancies us, we are in here."

"No way, I'm off," and with that, I legged it out of the block, eventually Tommy following, shouting "Wait!"

Clear of the area, I stopped running and let him catch up and straight away he said, "What the hell did you leave for?"

"Think about it," I said. "Why did she leave us at the bottom of the stairs before going up? She was up to something. I reckon she probably had a bloke up there telling him she's got a couple of young sailors with money in their pockets. I reckon we were gonna get mugged!"

He wouldn't have it, insisting that she fancied us

both and we've just missed out on a good time. Whatever and whoever was right, to this day we would never know who was right!

Not a good first footing on Italian soil and it just had to get worse. It came my way the following night when out with the 'big boys' for a rake around town. After a couple of bars, it was on to a late opening club that to me, was similar to where we had just been but a bit bigger with a much older clientele.

Needless to say after sticking it out for an hour or so I wanted to be off. Having drunk too much of things I'd never even heard of, it would be fair to say I was a bit worse for wear but was told to sit it out till we were all ready to leave. As they said, "You aint going back on your own and put that money away safe instead of sticking out of your shirt top pocket for all to see!"

I took the second bit of advice but as for the first, I'd had enough of the drink and the place so thought I would sneak away, which via the toilets wasn't difficult.

Outside I remembered their first bit of advice of keeping my money out of sight and transferred the

Lira to my sock and yes, believe it or not… coins as well! You do daft things when you are drunk!

Now with a profound 'coin' limp, fortunately I set off in the right direction following the basic sailors inbuilt compass of 'they always go down to the sea.' With the docks in the distance I had a wide road to navigate that was split with a tree lined island between the two sets of traffic and an ideal place to cross… or so I thought!

After reaching the island, the next is a bit of a blur, other than being on my knees with a sore head up against a tree. Then, as I became more aware, two quite old people were stood over me pointing and jabbering away furiously in Italian. With the back of my head throbbing more, I figured these were the ones who had hit me from behind. Fending them off and shouting at them as they came nearer I staggered across the road.

Taking a breather, I looked back to see if they were following me only to see them stood in the same place waving and pointing as if they were trying to tell me something.

At the first open dock gate I tried to explain to

the security what had happened but sticking the letter 'o' on the end of words like, "I've just been strucko on heado," My improvised Italian wasn't obviously working and all they were interested in was me producing my seaman's I.D card to allow me on to the dock.

Straight to my cabin bunk I went, and as the alcohol started to wear off, my forehead was now throbbing like the back of my head!

Soon the Chief Steward who doubled as our part time medic was summoned and began to pick little splinters from my forehead and checking out the bump at the back of my head, asked how it happened?

Fortunately, the 'old boys' had pre-briefed me and told me to say I had fallen a couple of times while drunk. Better than reporting an assault with the police and skipper getting involved, especially with the ship almost due to sail.

It wasn't worth the risk seeing as I was pretty much ok, with the only medical treatment needed being the Chief's paracetamol and a reminder from him that I still wasn't old enough to drink!

As the throbbing head eased, the night started to become clearer, coming to the conclusion that the couple were my saviors, having seen someone else whack me from behind before falling into the spiky barked tree, scaring the attacker off and that's what they were probably trying to tell me when I reached the other side of the road.

A bollocking followed from the guys I went out with having not listened to them about going back on my own but at least they saw the funny side when I told them my money stayed safe... coins and all, stuffed in me socks!

CHAPTER 9: ANOTHER TOUR AND TROUBLE AGAIN!

With what had gone on, I was glad to see the back of Italy and now with 1200 miles before Piraeus in Greece, time to reflect, thinking things could have turned out much worse than they did!

With the seagulls refusing to deliver newspapers it was down to the B.B.C. World Service radio to keep us in touch with what's going on back home and around the world.

Mobile phones and texting were still worlds away, so it was left to the tried and tested 'pen and parchment' method with air mail letters keeping everyone up to date.

One thing I wasn't going to divulge was the two Genoa episodes, believing what they don't know won't hurt them as I rushed through my latest update in time for posting in Greece.

Having wrote in the letter I fancied a trip to the age-old Acropolis ruins, as luck would have it Paddy must have been reading my mind and volunteered to be tour rep again. For that trip another cash sub was required and keeping those 50 years old pay sheets it's interesting to see that I withdrew 200 Drachma (£2 15s 7d) then but £26 now... how times have changed! Knowing absolutely nothing about its history, Paddy said not to worry he would tell us all we needed to know. That he certainly did, as well as every English-speaking tourist in earshot as he described in detail how its foundations were set in the Stoneage before the Romans took over.

Ancient Greece at its best. The Acropolis – but beware of your tour guide!

Realising that chiseling out stone pillars was not for them, they abandoned the project to go straight road building leaving it to the marauding Vikings who also got bored to go pillaging instead.

Finally, the Irish moved in with Whimpy's taking over but running out of money before finishing the roof and windows!

If only I could put into print the way he told it, this Irish banter went on for nearly an hour having everybody but the purists in fits of laughter. It was some history lesson cracking everyone up and a tale only he could tell!

A good day was had by all as we headed back to the ship and just two more ports of call before heading home.

Back to the bulkhead chart and at 590 miles to Famagusta, Cyprus was by comparison a short skip and a jump across the 'Med' and another country to tick off. As we took on the Cypriot tugs there was already plenty of traffic in port as they gently nudged us in at the end of half a dozen ships tied up stem to stern.

With the working day almost at an end, derricks had to be topped in readiness for the next day's unloading, leaving just a shower and change before another run ashore.

Saddled with clearing up after the P.O.'s had finished their evening meal, Tommy agreed to wait for me and with a probable long night ahead there was no need to rush.

It was a warm evening when we set off down the dock taking in who's in port from the berthed ships, acknowledging those sat out on deck as we passed, on our way to meet the others in the Harbour bar.

The pub was buzzing when we arrived, and one couldn't help noticing a line of some 30 plus beer mugs half full of lager, the other with froth as staff struggled with the filling.

As fast as they were corrected they were snaffled up by thirsty drinkers until this slow continuous beer line slowed even further. Eventually it was decided enough was enough of waiting, so off they went down town with us to meet them later. The slow topping up had suited Tommy and me fine until it stopped altogether, so we decided to try a drink we had never heard of - Brandy Sour!

Getting two large ones for the price of one proved the wrong choice second time around as I rushed to the door, making it to the street where I was sick as the proverbial dog!

As we sat on the kerb outside the bar, it was a no brainer deciding that back to the ship we must go but with my legs not doing what my head was telling them, Tommy's assistance was needed even though he wasn't in good shape himself.

At the dock gate Tommy asked those policing it if they could help by running us down in their jeep but was flatly refused, so walking was our only option. Having staggered past the guard house we had to stop and take a rest, only for Tommy to disappear amongst a load of farm machinery that had just been unloaded.

Next thing I knew he reappeared driving a tractor shouting "Get on the back quick!" and off we shot, tearing down the dock with cheers coming from the crews sitting out on deck who obviously saw the funny side. Coming to a halt, he shouted "Run Tiny!" as he legged it up the gangway but in a totally confused and semi drunken state, I was easy pickings for the chasing dock police who hauled me into their jeep and back to the guardhouse. Putting me into a small barred cell it then hit home that I was in real trouble now, especially when I was getting some smirky, creepy looks from the guy in charge!

It seemed I'd been locked up for hours before I heard familiar voices outside arguing with the chief as to why their taxi couldn't take them right to the ship. I made sure they knew I was inside by shouting out as loud as I could.

In they thankfully came, demanding to know why I was behind bars regardless of what I'd done. As more started to arrive back from town, the small guardroom was filling up. As they continued to argue the point that a young lad should not be behind bars they somehow negotiated to keep me in the guard room but not locked up.

The more they made a commotion the more frustrated the chief became and to clear his guard room, agreed to ferry everyone to the ship. What happened next Steve McQueen would have been proud of in the 'Great Escape,' as I was man handled behind the bodies in the overcrowded guard room out into an open back truck, seats down both sides, me laid on the floor with legs covering over me and a few extra bodies on top!

With still plenty of guys left arguing for the sake

of it to cause a distraction in the guard room, they still hadn't missed me as we set off down the dock, thankful that I wouldn't be spending the night in the cell but knowing this probably won't be the end of the matter!

And so it proved as I was summoned to see the Captain next morning along with the police chief. One person you don't mess with is the Captain of a ship who is Lord and Master, judge and jury. Told to reveal the name of the tractor driver, I had no choice but to come clean.

Fortunately, however, a compromise was found when the police agreed to waive this indiscretion seeing no damage was done, providing there was no more bother the second and final night we were in port. Should there be then they would return for me and Tommy.

In no uncertain terms the skipper made it clear that Tommy and I would not be allowed ashore while here in Famagusta, though to be honest I wouldn't have gone anyway!

No gripes came from Tommy when I told him I had no choice but to 'sprag' on him and he even said we should take over the gangway duty that night and remind everyone who goes ashore to behave themselves. Would they take any notice from two of the most junior on board? Only time would tell!

In between seeing off the guys going ashore, we filled the early hours in with him beating me in every game of table tennis but come midnight we were back on the gangway to sit, wait and hope!

We didn't have to wait too long before the first back said they had heard that two seamen had stolen a push bike, one croggying the other. When stopped, they threw it at the copper but were eventually arrested and taken to the main police station!

As more came back they asked us, was it true that our galley boy had been arrested for breaking into a dock side cabin and stealing a load of cigarettes? Surely not, we thought, as cigs were for next to nowt from our own duty-free bond… why would he need to do something daft like that?

True or not, he still wasn't back on board, but it was enough for me to press the panic button and think of nothing other than me being arrested. So, without a word to anyone I was off, deciding to hide in a forward locker while working out what to do next and try and get myself out of this serious, stupid mess!

I soon came to the conclusion that my options were few, with the best being to stay hidden till the ship sails then when away from the port, give myself up to the Captain and take what punishment he hands out.

This, I thought, was better than being taken off the ship by the police, being locked up, probably prosecuted, flown home at my expense, then finally the big one; a D.R. (Decline to Report) in my Discharge Book and kicked out of the Merchant Navy!! What a bloody mess!!!

Stuffed up inside the locker, no water, or food and minus my watch so no recollection of time, the plan now was to only emerge after the sound of the screws turning.

All that was keeping me going was the thought that the longer I could stay in here the less chance the police would find me. Eventually it was music to my ears when the banging of the hatch lids closing meant that departure couldn't be too far off.

Desperate for a drink, I just had to tough it out for a little longer, though with the temperature rising inside it needed to come sooner rather than later as I was really starting to struggle.

"I've cracked it," I thought when I heard the sound of our twin screws turning over, meaning we were on our way. Now all I had to do was wait a little longer to get rid of the pilot and tugs then... Bingo! I'm out of here!

Disaster!

It's a massive false call. After 15 minutes or so, the engines suddenly stopped, and I could feel the motion of the ship doing likewise. Something was wrong, this isn't supposed to happen but enough was enough cooped up in my metal prison and I just had to get out, whatever the outcome!

As I walked out onto the foredeck nobody seemed to notice me with attentions elsewhere, people leaning over the side and it wasn't till I got inside the midships accommodation that the call went out.

"The little bugger's here!"

"We're going back in," someone shouted. The

tug had left it too late to release the aft hawser and its now got wrapped round one of the props.

"Shit," just my luck, now it could be curtains for me if they come back before a diver is called out to cut us free.

After a welcome shower, downing pints of water as if they were going out of fashion, an expected bollocking off the bosun followed. Surprisingly, a visit up top to see the skipper was thankfully avoided when unbeknown to him I hadn't gone missing, with the deck guys reasoning I'd be on the ship somewhere and not done a runner ashore before she sailed.

But what about the trouble makers?

The bike thieves were British seamen… but off another ship. And as for our cig stealing galley boy, he was a case of mistaken identity. Someone off our ship had seen a similar looking guy being put in a police van and again, putting two and two together and getting five!

Unbelievable! Absolutely unbelievable! You honestly couldn't make it up. All that for what? Nothing!!!

CHAPTER 10:
HOME RUN

Six hours later we were on our way again. Roll on Barcelona, surely nothing can happen there!

It was a good hike to Spain; 1600 miles, nearly the full length of the 'Med' giving us plenty of time to finish off painting the ship from top to bottom. With the hull paint job started in Famagusta it was planned to be finished in this, our last port before London.

Having done a big chunk of the starboard hull we were now port side to the dock and Tommy and I were down to do the midships section away from where the cargo was being slung.

"No pratting about you two," was the bosun's orders as we rigged our stage, lashing on our paint trays and pots. Lowering the stage was done by easing the rope turns on the ends of the stage causing it to go down in controlled gentle jerks before making good again.

We however, fancying ourselves as the 'A Team' used a faster method, though definitely not in the seaman's manual.

Being distracted from above and not paying full attention to the job in hand, I whipped off all the turns while gripping a wrong loose end causing the stage to collapse at my end sending it into a violent pendulum swinging motion.

This left Tommy hanging on grimly, me underneath him upside down with my legs fortunately somehow over the horns of the stage like the catcher on a trapeze act!

As crew and dock workers rushed to our aid it wasn't till later they told me my head was missing the dock side bollard by mere inches as it swung back and forth. With me upside down, the black and white gloss paint duly followed, covering me all over even inside one of my ears!

Unhitching me off the stage, my legs were like jelly being assisted up the gangway, the guys telling me how bloody lucky I was not to have smashed my head in on that bollard.

Having lived to tell the tale, next job was to get the paint removed which was by far no simple task and by the time all was scrubbed off using cotton waste and turps I looked like a cherry tomato - and a sore one at that!

Staying in port just 30 hours, those half dozen steps to the gangway would be the only ones on Spanish soil but I couldn't help thinking how lucky I was. Or should that be unlucky?

Thinking back to what old Sam said about the Albatross and bad luck coming our way, well that bird must have been eyeing up me in particular! Lost the camera in Auckland, could have been mugged twice in Genoa, locked up in Famagusta then nearly killed here! I think I've had more than my fair share!

However, on the other hand, some believe the Albatross brings on a 'fair wind' and with it, good luck.

So other than losing that damn camera all the other instances could have turned out so much worse... the jury is therefore still out on this contentious Albatross saga!

The last leg would be a further 1800 miles before London with only the Bay of Biscay to possibly worry about. Known for some of the Atlantics fiercest weather we hit it at its mildest, far from its reputation of a graveyard for shipping over the years. Having sailed nearly 31,000 miles it was into the channel, then the Thames and as we passed the Gravesend Sea School for a second time it was hard to believe it was only 4 months 24 days ago that we first sailed by!

It had been some journey, a great experience one that I would never have missed. Visiting seven countries, the highs far out-scoring the lows but there was still one outstanding thing left to do.

The baker's camera!

Leaving it to the very last minute - that being the pay-off table - I finally came clean with the lads who, after calling me a right numpty or words to that effect, said pay him what he paid and no more.

Still dreading the moment, surprisingly he took it very well saying he only bought it as an investment and figured awhile back something had gone amiss. Phew! Didn't expect that! Neither did I expect the size of my first ever wage, earning £227 13s 9d (£2752.55 at today's rates) which was some pay off for a 16-year-old who enjoyed it that much that I put my name down to return for the next voyage and do it all over again... well maybe not all!

EPILOGUE

Following 24 days paid leave (one day for every week at sea), it was back down to London and the Cretic, sailing to:- Panama, New Zealand, Cyprus, Greece, Italy, France and Southampton. Then 7 more voyages:

PACIFIC STRONGHOLD:- London, Leith, Glasgow, Panama, West Coast America, Canada, London.

MEGANTIC: -Hull, Norway, Finland, Sweden, Holland, Tyne-and-Wear.

RUBENS:- Liverpool, Cardiff.

CASTILLIAN:- Hull, West Coast Africa, Immingham.

DUMURRA (3 voyages):- Liverpool, West Coast Africa, Avonmouth.

ACKNOWLEDGEMENTS

A big thank you to Catherine without whose help this book may not have been published. Also a rap for 'Big' John and not forgetting dear wife Ann who had so much to put up with during its making!

N.B. To all family and friends who haven't bought a copy - no worries as you've probably heard these tales many times before!

Printed in Great Britain
by Amazon